BABY ANIMALS

STICKER ACTIVITY BOOK

How to use this book:

- Pull out the sticker sheets and keep them by you when you look at each page.

- Read the words on the page and look at the shapes. Can you see a sticker that fits?

- When you have found the right sticker, carefully peel it off and stick it on the page.

- Have fun!

Let's go wild!

Find the animals who are playing in the hot SUN today!

I have lots of stripes. Find me!

Find me!

I like to hide in the grass.

Add more **butterflies!**

Look at me, everyone!

I have red and blue wings.

My best friend is Zebra.

I love to cuddle with Mom!

I have blue wings.

Can you find all my bug friends?
There are 10 of us!

5

Find me!

Double trouble!

striped is best!

Striped

Colorful kids!
Find the busy babies and see who's the cutest.

I love to play!

striped balls are FUN!

I can run fast.

Can you find our brothers?

Spotted

Find us!

6

7

Puppy play!

Guess which puppy has found the ball.

How many puppies are there on this page?

Stickers for pages 2 and 3

Stickers for pages 4 and 5

Stickers for pages 6 and 7

tickers for paaes 12 and 13

tickers for pages 10 and 11

tickers for page 16

Well done! 5 found!

Maze fun

Help Maisy find her mom,
but watch out for the
cheeky chicks on the way!

EXIT!

Start here!

9

Complete the scene and have FUN!

Search the
scene. Try
to find ...

2 calves

3 piglets

1 foal

4 lambs

6 chicks

2 kids

Farm fun!

15

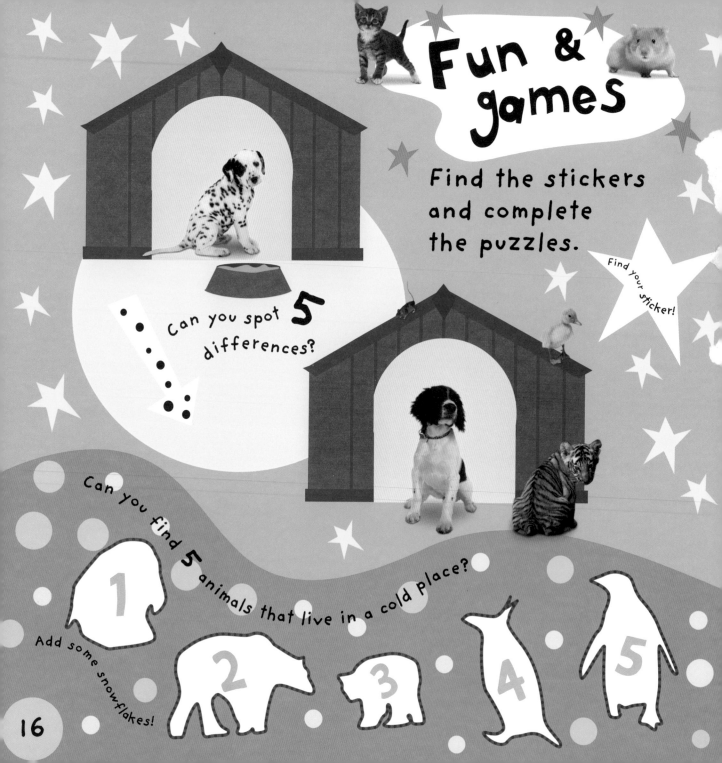

Fun & games

Find the stickers and complete the puzzles.

Find your sticker!

Can you spot **5** *differences?*

Can you find **5** *animals that live in a cold place?*

Add some snowflakes!

1

2

3

4

5

16